MEMORY KEEPER

Aleksandar Duravcevic

ORDOVAS

INTRODUCTION

Pilar Ordovas

I met Aleksandar Duravcevic through a common friend in September 2015. Before our first meeting, this friend had shown me some of his work; I then got to know Aleksandar and first fell in love with the beauty and intimacy of his drawings, and then, through multiple studio visits, discovered his paintings, sculptures and films. From the winter of 2015 I have lived with some of his drawings in my office at the gallery, which I see every day when I am in London.

Last spring we started talking about this exhibition, his first show in London. In the months that followed we selected the work together and **Memory Keeper** started to take shape.

Saša is a wonderful storyteller. His works have explored his concerns with identity and his own history and are deeply personal, but resonate with so many of us. It is partly as a foreigner who has lived outside my country for more than half of my life that I relate to his concerns, but it is also because they are universal, speaking to the humanity and personal experience in all of us. His strong ties with Montenegro and the tradition of telling stories and keeping the memory for other generations, inspired the title of this exhibition.

The artist's studio, New York, detail

Since I have known Saša, he has sometimes sent me texts of great authors he felt were relevant to our conversations; or images will land in my phone, full of rainbows and sometimes feathers – which is one of my obsessions and first brought me to his work. Through found images we know well, like the double rainbow on the Victoria Falls, he creates images in black and white, prepared in the same way as Byzantine icon paintings, or on paper, exploring the idea that neither memory nor the reproduction of a memory can ever be the same as the real thing. This exhibition includes a range of such works, as well as sculpture and one of his films.

I hope you all enjoy it as much as I have enjoyed working with Saša.

Thank you to Xavier Salomon and Phong Bui for their wonderful contributions to the catalogue and above all thank you to you, Saša.

Aleksandar Duravcevic, *Touch me not*, 2017 (detail)

UPON VISITING
THE ARTIST'S STUDIO
(DEORVM-MANIVM-
IVRA-SANCTA-SVNTO)

Xavier F. Salomon, Asolo, Easter 2017

HIC
IACET
PVLVIS
CINIS
ET
NIHIL

Qual fia ristoro a' dì perduti un sasso
Che distingua le mie dalle infinite
Ossa che in terra e in mar semina morte? [1]

In December 1646, Cardinal Antonio Barberini, Pope Urban VIII's younger brother, died in Rome and was buried in the church of the Capuchins, the order he belonged to. As a member of the immediate papal family his body was interred in front of the high altar of the church, but with typical Capuchin simplicity, he had dictated his epitaph: HIC IACET PVLVIS CINIS ET NIHIL. Here lies dust, ashes, and nothing.

In the mountains of Montenegro a cemetery is fashioned around nameless stones that mark the burial places of ancestors. Names are not needed, because the families know who is buried there. A stone is placed, as a sign, to activate our memory.

In London, in the early 1920s, in the aftermath of World War I, a monument was erected to an unknown soldier. A single, unrecognisable body, from one of the French battlefields of the Western Front, was picked at random and then buried in Westminster Abbey. A black stone slab was inscribed: 'Beneath this stone rests the body of a British warrior unknown by name or rank brought from France to lie among the most illustrious of the land…Thus are commemorated the many multitudes

o of Cardinal Antonio Barberini in the Church of the Immacolata Concezione, Rome. Fondo Edifici di Culto, Ministero dell'Interno.

who during the Great War of 1914–1918 gave the most that man can give, life itself, for God, for King and country, for loved ones, home and empire, for the sacred cause of justice and the freedom of the world. They buried him among the kings because he had done good toward God and toward his house.' A single tomb of a single soldier thus stood for the millions who died in World War I, and in any previous or subsequent war. This single example was then repeated in the capitals of most world countries.

Sepulchres, monuments, urns, tombstones, sarcophagi, cenotaphs mark the resting place or memorialise the dead. They are usually made of stone. Local, unassuming, stones, sometimes exotic and outlandish. Stone is used, inscribed (or even left blank), sculpted and polished to defy time and loss. Words are set in stone, because paper is often too insubstantial. And so, like a nameless grave, a book without words can record words and stories that are not necessarily written on it. A large stone book in Tuscan travertine, because books, like tombs, connect us to the past, to something that is long gone, but that we can evoke. A blank stone book, or a stack of unadorned urns, trigger reminiscences from the past – distant or not so distant – memories of people, places, and experiences. They become collective, they become vessels that contain the ashes of all our dead, and books that contain all the words we have written.

In the summer of 1806, the Italian poet Ugo Foscolo responded to the Napoleonic Edict of Saint-Cloud, which prohibited bodies from being buried within city walls and prescribed that cemeteries should be established in the outskirts of cities, by composing a poem, titled 'Dei Sepolcri'. Foscolo started by asking if the existence of tombs would make death any less painful: *'All'ombra de' cipressi e dentro l'urne / confortate di pianto è forse il sonno / della morte men duro?'* [2] For Foscolo tombs were significant as markers of great figures of the past. In the poem, he describes walking around Santa Croce in Florence, being inspired by the monuments to Machiavelli, Michelangelo, Galileo, and Alfieri (*'A egregie cose il forte animo accendono / l'urne de' forti'* [3]). Tombs are not important as containers of bodies, but as containers of memories and of past deeds. What happened in Troy was chronicled because of Homer's account in the *Iliad*; Foscolo imagined the ancient poet visiting the tombs of his heroes, embracing their urns and interrogating them – *'Un dì vedrete / mendico un cieco errar sotto le vostre / antichissime ombre, e brancolando / penetrar negli avelli, e abbracciar l'urne, / e interrogarle.'* [4]

E l'estreme sembianze e le reliquie
Della terra e del ciel traveste il tempo [5]

Pontormo's Santa Felicita *Deposition*. Mark Rothko's recipe for a work
of art ('1. There must be a clear preoccupation with death – intimations
of mortality… Tragic art, romantic art etc. deals with the knowledge
of death'). Caravaggio's *Boy with a Basket of Fruit*. A litany of family
names across the centuries, from 'Ivani' to 'Augustin'. Velázquez's *Los
borrachos*. A black and white photograph of an execution during the
Spanish Civil War. John Cage's rules and hints for students and teachers
('Save everything. It may come in handy later'). A silver ex-voto of a leg
– stained and blackened.

Repetition is part of a mnemonic exercise. On the walls graphite
drawings on black paper. A series of identical, and yet individual,
images. Diptychs and pairs. Each piece fiercely singular in its repetitive
conception. Byzantine icons have always been about repetition. From
Constantinople to Novgorod, they reiterate the same religious images
throughout time – images which are not man-made. Every single icon,
however, is a tool for different types of worship. Everyone in front of
an icon has a different emotional response. And everyone responds
to nature, as well as to the sacred, in diverse manners. Victoria Falls,

the same image of water falling in everlasting replication (yet always different water; never the same). Painted on an icon board, Victoria Falls become the present Nikopeia, the Hodegetria of global life.

Candles are lit in front of icons in churches. And candles also always look identical, but they are replaced every day. With every candle that is consumed a human supplication vanishes. A drawing can be made in the breath of a candle's lifespan. Like an ancient icon, each stroke, each line, each mark is a monastic act, an offering. Now the candles are electrical, and each prayer can be reutilized. But they flicker in silver and even though they have lost their wax body, they shine in the darkness of the paper, automated tools of an ancient practice. Metal, mineral signs on a flat sheet. Here Byzantine severity joins Florentine grace.

A withered laurel wreath and a taxidermy owl. Also stones and trees. Everything in the studio is a relic. Vestiges, like tombs and inscriptions, of the past. Material traces of memories and feelings. Because everything will be 'dust, ashes, and nothing', and, as Foscolo writes 'time overpowers the extreme forms and the relics of earth and heaven.' As human beings we are given one tool: to remember and to be remembered. *'Celeste è questa / corrispondenza d'amorosi sensi, / celeste dote è negli umani.'* [6] This allows us to connect to the past and project into the future. Humans are born with the awareness of their temporality.

Like a sheet of paper, a black surface – a door – is covered in nimble lines. They coil, they travel across the surface. Pools of silver colour sparkle, each line is a memory of something, each reflection of the colour a link to a vanished emotion that can fleetingly resurface. Ephemeral lines that move with the imperceptible wind that comes from the street. The movement so insignificant that it is barely observable. Time moves its inexorable fingers over this relic too. *'Requiem aeternam, dona eis, Domine, et lux perpetua luceat eis.'* [7]
A silvery feather.

[1] What comfort for the lost days will a stone be / setting apart mine from the countless bones / that death disseminates in sea and earth?*

[2] Under the shadow of the cypress trees / within the urns wetted by loving tears / can the slumber of death be less profound?*

[3] The tombs of great men do spur the great souls / to noble deeds*

[4] One day you will see / a blind beggarly person wander here / under your ancient shadow, grope his way / into the deep-set tombs, and clasp the urns, / and question them.*

[5] All that is left / is transformed by the ceaseless flow of time*

[6] It is divine, / this dialogue of love, / a divine gift in human beings*

[7] Eternal rest grant unto them O Lord, and let perpetual light shine upon them.

* All translations of Foscolo's 'Dei Sepolcri' are from *Rediscovering Foscolo: A Translation of The 'Sepolcri' and of Three Sonnets*, unpublished manuscript by Valentina Bianchi, University of Siena, available at https://unisi.academia.edu/ValentinaBianchi

Aleksandar Duravcevic, *Touch me not*, 2017

ALEKSANDAR DURAVCEVIC: THE NECESSARY REVERIE

Phong Bui

They rose to where their sovereign eagle sails,
They kept their faith, their freedom, on the height,
Chaste, frugal, savage, arm'd by and day and night…
O smallest peoples! rough rockthrone
Of Freedom!

— ALFRED LORD TENNYSON, *MONTENEGRO* [1] —

Albanians thought I was Montenegrin
Montenegrins thought I was Albanian
Italians thought I was a Slav
Latinos think I am Italian
Blacks think I am French
French think I am one of their own.

— ALEKSANDAR DURAVCEVIC —

Aleksandar Duravcevic, *Waiting*, 2015 (film still)

Aleksandar Duravcevic, *Identity*, 2015, Montenegrin Pavilion at La Biennale di Venezia, 56th International Art Exhibition

ALBANIANS THOUGHT I WAS MONTENEGRIN

MONTENEGRINS THOUGHT I WAS ALBANIAN

ITALIANS THOUGHT I WAS A SLAV

LATINOS THINK I AM ITALIAN

BLACKS THINK I AM FRENCH

FRENCH THINK I AM ONE OF THEIR OWN

During the Balkan crisis Montenegro caught the attention of Alfred Lord Tennyson, British Poet Laureate, who was regarded as the most famous writer of the Victorian age. His poem *Montenegro* pays tribute to the fierce but few Montenegrin warriors – 'O smallest among peoples' – fighting against the large Turkish army, and uses a repertoire of poetic devices to associate Montenegro with the 'rough rock-throne of Freedom'. Tennyson's poem stands as testament to the complex history of the small country of Montenegro, and the fact that – due largely to its desirable geographic position between the East and the West – its past is inseparable from its turbulent history of wars.

Those who have followed Aleksandar Duravcevic's work are likely to detect two distinct but coexisting attributes that relate to both the notion of Volksgeist, 'the spirit of the people' and a sense of dislocation. 'In his oeuvre,' first of all, as Daria Filardo wrote, 'the history of Montenegro is not rendered through an anthropological and documentary approach, but it transpires from the autobiographical past of the artist.'[2] In other words, being receptive to the 'spirit of the people' or 'people's culture' involves accepting that everything about an individual is to some degree a creation of others before him or her as well as his or her contemporaries. This condition embodies Duravcevic's worldview as an artist, enabling him to unfold his expansive rapport with the history of Montenegro as well as his personal history.

For Duravcevic, experience itself is buffeted by personal memory and the complex intermingling of identity and cultural history. Like many exiles who experience themselves in the liminal space between the local and global, between the personal and universal, between national traditions and Western culture, Duravcevic is constantly crossing boundaries. In line with the demands of exile, Duravcevic is unremittingly aware of what he needs to keep and what he must leave behind – repetition and excess become existential. Repetition stems from the need to retell narratives over and over again from their beginnings in order to recover memories – symbolically reconstituting a full reality from the small fragments that can be transported. It can also be seen as a form of excess that carves out a feasible space for the exile that resists the many circumscribing pressures that otherwise restrict him or her. It is therefore in the space between repetition and excess where parallels and opposites emerge, that Duravcevic finds a unique mechanism for lessening the weight of his cultural burden, distributing one half of the load in Montenegro and the other half in the U.S.

While his works can be seen as autobiographical memories, episodic recollections, based on an amalgam of personal experiences, general knowledge, and facts about the world, they also refer to an involuntary sense of memory in which past episodes surface without conscious effort.

Aleksandar Duravcevic, *Mother*, 2009–14, Contemporary Art Center of Montenegro

In his serial drawing entitled *EMPIRE*, 2013–2017, images of an eagle in profile – drawn with subtle differences from one to another – recall the eagle at the end of Tennyson's opening line, a universal emblem of strength, power and vision. In this case it also refers to the national symbols of Montenegro, Duravcevic's old homeland, America, his adopted home, and, equally importantly, to his one year of military service in the now defunct Yugoslav Army and subsequent flight (by boat) to Florence, Italy. Similarly, the stacked zinc buckets in *Mother*, 2009 –14, and the stacked wooden urns in *Monument to the unknown hero*, 2016, contain references to both the public and private sphere, recalling Constantin Brancusi's *Endless Column*, 1918, and the minimalist's serial use of modules. Simultaneously, the first contemplates the bucket as a readymade object as well as being a personal homage to the artist's mother, who became a house cleaner when she arrived in New York City in 1992. Meanwhile, the second, a made object, pays universal homage to fallen heroes, while its form and materials evoke the strong, masculine military archetype that Duravcevic encountered during his military service. At the same time metallic particles in the urns' glaze refract a hallucinatory, rainbow-like light, which blur the conditions of dreaming and remembrance.

Aleksandar Duravcevic, *Monument to the unknown hero*, 2016 (detail)

Duravcevic's particular deployment of repetition or serialisation conforms neither to the typically Eastern use of repetition to transcend materiality, as in a mantra, nor to the typically Western use of repetition as manifestation of wealth, power, and abundance, as in the mass produced goods that one sees displayed in a supermarket. Duravcevic's multiples are drenched in issues of remembering, remapping, retreading, and retracing his own history and culture while challenging false claims of hierarchy and hegemony, even false affirmations of identity. His process of multiplicity is dialectical and unpredictable. In *Touch me not*, 2017, and *Electric Souls*, 2015, subtle resonances of metaphor and material intersect. *Touch me not* is an open book that signifies education, knowledge and wisdom; it is made of travertine marble. *Electric Souls* is a symbol of light in the darkness of the life and light in the next world; the drawn candle looks soft on simple, black paper. Gaston Bachelard has written beautifully on the dialectic of hard and soft:

> 'In the language of matter, *yes* and *no* are translated as soft and hard. No images of matter exist outside this dialectic of invitation and exclusion, a dialectic which the imagination transposes into countless metaphors – a dialectic even known at times to invert itself under the influence of a curious ambivalence, to the point where it may impute a hypocritical hostility to softness, a provocative invitingness to hardness.'[3]

Aleksandar Duravcevic, *Electric Souls*, 2015 (detail)

The artist's personal idiom of seriality continues in *Double Life* (two modest-sized oil paintings in black and white, of a view of Victoria Falls on the Zambezi River at the border of Zambia and Zimbabwe). The interplay between two identical paintings becomes a pun on the notion of a double life, from one person who has dual identities, and from an image of water. Like fire, earth, and air, water is a vital substance – integral to our physical universe – and is a symbol that inhabits our dreams and reveries. Under a close inspection, minute differences in the painting are visible, in spite of the artist's wish to create identical twins. Furthermore, there are two tendencies that underlie Duravcevic's dual aspirations: one, his desire to make representational painting in the manner of the sublime that offers him occasional culverts to art history as optional digressions from avant-garde practice; two, the choice of this specific waterfall also calls upon the ethos of paradise lost and the value of reverie. Victoria Falls is a desirable destination that Duravcevic may aspire to experience in reality, yet by substituting it with a poetic image which must be made physical, he proposes a subtle distinction between reverie and dreaming: whereas a dream can lose some of its potency once it has been realised, reverie preserves that distance from realisation, creating a romantic condition of repose. As Bachelard suggested, 'it is a phenomenon of solitude which has its roots in the soul of the dreamer. … [Cosmic reveries] situate us in a world and not in a society.' [4]

Aleksandar Duravcevic, *Double Life*, 2017

Aleksandar Duravcevic, *Double Life*, 2017

Perhaps the difference between being in society and being in the world is the collapse of the past into the future, which manifests as an intensified preoccupation with the moment. What if the preoccupation of the moment is the confluence of the future of the reflection and the reflected? *Waiting*, 2015, a twenty-minute loop video depicting an older Montenegrin woman waiting for something to occur, is a pristine encapsulation. One is reminded of Henri Bergson's remark on the basic difference between perception and reflection that constructs every living moment:

> 'Every moment of our life presents two aspects, it is actual and virtual, perception on the one side and memory on the other. Each moment of life is split up as and when it is posited. Or rather, it consists in this very splitting, for the present moment, always going forward, fleeting limit between the immediate past which is now no more and the immediate future which is not yet, would be a mere abstraction were it not the moving mirror which continually reflects perception as a memory.'[5]

Perhaps the older woman is a presentation of optimism and pessimism? Ralph Waldo Emerson would attest to the first, 'The philosophy of waiting is sustained by all the oracles of the universe,'[6] while Samuel Beckett the second, 'The end is in the beginning and yet you go on.'[7] Those of us who have observed horizontally expanding and intensifying capitalism, especially through the rapid dominance of technology, are aware of its inherent indifference to the future, and the protrusion of the 'now' into the past and future. Most definitely, all of us are also aware of how our ability for self-contemplation has been eroded. Hence we're inevitably influenced by its pace, and as a result, are losing our ability to communicate to each other. As Duravcevic once expressed, 'one of the reasons why people resist technology, or push for homogeneity, globalization, or obliterate boundaries by asserting themselves through the names of their gods, it's still here with us.'[8] One can think of Duravcevic's deity as his art, which embraces time as one unified simultaneity. Every work he has made is a product of his thoughtful meditation. Whether through the language of traditional art, modernism and postmodernism, or his emphasis of the handmade – whether by his hands or those of an artisan – he is engaged in a constant, deliberate drive toward repose: a condition wherein the voluntary and involuntary senses of memory are timelessly suspended in space. Being away from the homeland seems to have fashioned in Duravcevic a poetic reverie that retrieves a universal sphere from personal accord, where time is endlessly intermingled.

1 Alfred, Lord Tennyson, *The Complete Poetical Works of Alfred, Lord Tennyson, Poet Laureate*, Harper & Brothers, 1884, p. 394.

2 Daria Filardo, 'Permanent Refugees' catalogue essay in *Ti Ricordi Sjecaš Li Se You Remember*, Centre of Contemporary Art of Montenegro, 2015, pp. 23 – 25.

3 Gaston Bachelard (trans. Kenneth Haltman), *Earth and Reveries of Will*, The Dallas Institute Publications, 2002, p. 13.

4 Gaston Bachelard, *The Poetics of Reverie: Childhood, Language, and the Cosmos*, Beacon Press, 1971, p. 14.

5 Henri Bergson, *Henri Bergson: Key Writings*, A&C Black, 2002, p. 147.

6 Ralph Waldo Emerson, *The Journals and Miscellaneous Notebooks of Ralph Waldo Emerson, Volume 11*, Harvard University Press, 1975, p. 15.

7 Samuel Beckett, *Endgame*, 1957. Accessed at http://samuel-beckett.net/endgame.html

8 Phong Bui, 'Aleksandar Duravcevic in Conversation with Phong Bui', *The Brooklyn Rail*, June, 2015.

Aleksandar Duravcevic, *Double Life*, 2017 (detail)

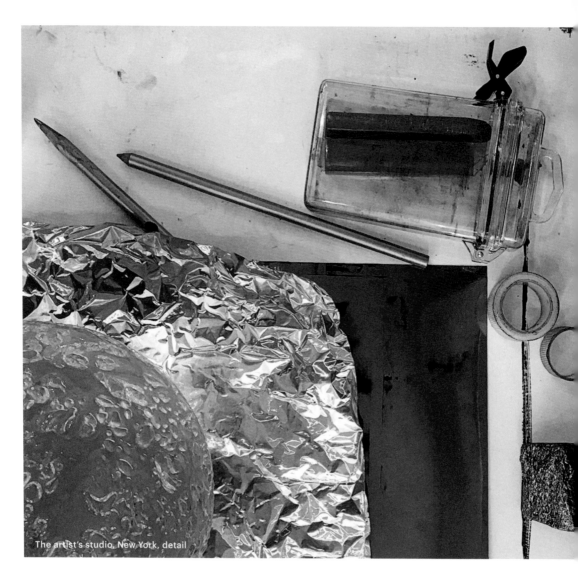
The artist's studio, New York, detail

ALEKSANDAR DURAVCEVIC
Double Life, 2017

ALEKSANDAR DURAVCEVIC
Double Life, 2017

ALEKSANDAR DURAVCEVIC
Double Life, 2017

ALEKSANDAR DURAVCEVIC
Touch me not, 2017

ALEKSANDAR DURAVCEVIC
Monument to the unknown hero, 2016

ALEKSANDAR DURAVCEVIC
Waiting, 2015

ALEKSANDAR DURAVCEVIC
Electric Souls, 2015

LIST OF
WORKS

Aleksandar Duravcevic

(b. 1970)

42–43
Double Life
oil on board
14 × 11 in. (35.5 × 27.9 cm.)
Painted in 2017

44–45
Double Life
diptych—oil on board
each: 11 × 14 in. (27.9 × 35.5 cm.)
Painted in 2017

46–47
Double Life
diptych—oil on board
each: 14 × 11 in. (35.5 × 27.9 cm.)
Painted in 2017

48–49
Touch me not
travertine with steel base
32¼ in. (82.5 cm.) high
Executed in 2017

50–51
Monument to the unknown hero
six lacquered wooden urns with stone pedestal
122½ in. (311.1 cm.) high
Executed in 2016

52–53
Waiting
Film
20 minutes
Executed in 2015
This work is from an edition of three

54–55
Electric Souls
graphite on paper
29 × 40 in. (73.6 × 101.6 cm.)
Executed in 2015

Published on the occasion of the exhibition
Memory Keeper: Aleksandar Duravcevic

9 June – 29 July 2017

ORDOVAS
25 SAVILE ROW LONDON W1S 2ER
T +44 (0)20 7287 5013
WWW.ORDOVASART.COM

Editor: Pilar Ordovas
Project managers: Kristen Force, Georgina Rumbellow,
Clara Zevi, Gonzalo Ordovás, Clare Roberts and Ria Kirby
Copy editor: Liane Jones

Design by Sinéad Madden
Printed in England by Pureprint, Uckfield

ISBN 978-0-9930843-7-9

Photography: cover and pages 5, 16, 17, 18,
30, 31, 33, 34, 35, 39, 43, 45,
49, 51, 55 and 60: photography by Mike Bruce; page 8:
© Roberto Apa; pages 13 and 28: © John Calabrese;
pages 23, 26 and 27: © Duško Miljanic.

We would like to extend our profound thanks to
Phong Bui, Ysabel Pinyol, Xavier F. Salomon
and David Totah for all their time and willingness to help,
as well as for their important
contributions to this exhibition.

A special thanks to Saša.

Aleksandar Duravcevic, *Touch me not*, 2017